MW00716662

The Long Trip West

by Joseph Blaire
illustrated by Tom McNeely

PEARSON

Scott
Foresman

Editorial Offices: Glenview, Illinois • Parsippany, New Jersey • New York, New York
Sales Offices: Needham, Massachusetts • Duluth, Georgia • Glenview, Illinois
Coppell, Texas • Ontario, California • Mesa, Arizona

Every effort has been made to secure permission and provide appropriate credit for photographic material. The publisher deeply regrets any omission and pledges to correct errors called to its attention in subsequent editions.

Unless otherwise acknowledged, all photographs are the property of Scott Foresman, a division of Pearson Education.

Illustrations by Tom McNeely

ISBN: 0-328-13415-5

Copyright © Pearson Education, Inc.

All Rights Reserved. Printed in the United States of America. This publication is protected by Copyright, and permission should be obtained from the publisher prior to any prohibited reproduction, storage in a retrieval system, or transmission in any form by any means, electronic, mechanical, photocopying, recording, or likewise. For information regarding permission(s), write to: Permissions Department, Scott Foresman, 1900 East Lake Avenue, Glenview, Illinois 60025.

7 8 9 10 V0G1 14 13 12 11 10 09 08

In 1803 Thomas Jefferson was president of the United States. At that time the United States was smaller than it is today. Much of the land west of the Mississippi River had been owned by Spain. But in 1800, Spain had given the land to France. Jefferson wanted to buy the land from France.

President Thomas Jefferson

On April 30, 1803, the leader of France agreed to sell this land to the United States. The deal was called the Louisiana Purchase. It doubled the size of the United States.

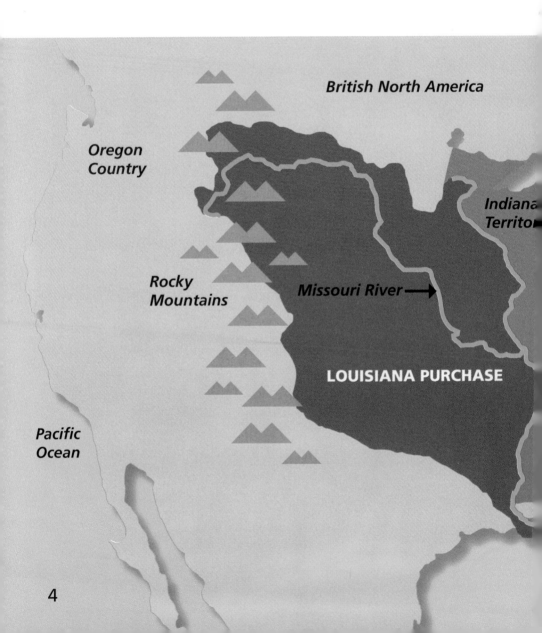

Jefferson knew that Americans would begin **migrating,** or moving. They would move from east to west into the land the country got in the Louisiana Purchase. This new territory, or area, spanned west from the Mississippi River to the Rocky Mountains. It spanned south from British North America to the Gulf of Mexico.

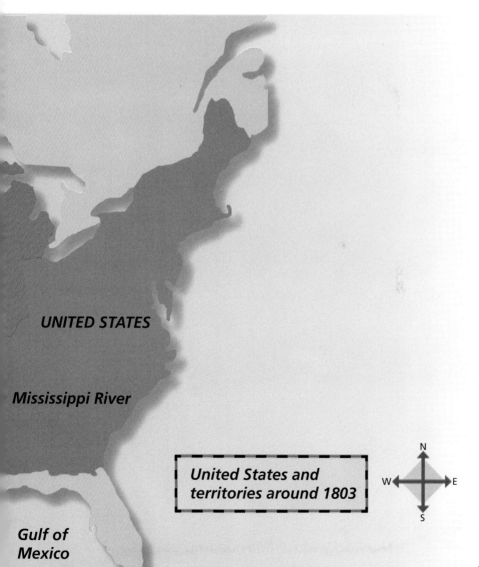

UNITED STATES

Mississippi River

United States and territories around 1803

N
W E
S

Gulf of Mexico

In 1803 President Jefferson also created the Corps of Discovery. The Corps of Discovery was a team led by Meriwether Lewis and William Clark. The team's job was to find and write about the rivers, mountains, animals, and Native American nations of the American West. The team's goal was to reach the Pacific Ocean.

The Rocky Mountains lie to the west.

Lewis and Clark, more than forty-five other people, and Lewis's black Newfoundland dog named Seaman became the Corps of Discovery. President Jefferson gave them the money they needed for their trip.

The Corps of Discovery loads trip supplies.

On May 14, 1804, the Corps of Discovery left the **wharf** of Camp Dubois in what is now Illinois. They began the long trip westward on the Missouri River. The trip was difficult. Some of the men became ill. It was also very hot. Clark made many maps. Lewis studied plants and animals. He took notes and made simple drawings of his discoveries.

The Corps of Discovery sets sail toward the west on the Missouri River.

The group met many Native Americans. Lewis and Clark needed to be able to talk and trade with the Native Americans. A woman named Sacagawea helped them. She was part of the Native American Shoshone nation. She **translated.** She also helped the group find plants to eat. She knew the land and helped guide the trip.

Sacagawea translates for Lewis and Clark.

On May 26, 1805, Lewis **scanned** the horizon. He saw the Rocky Mountains for the first time. They were rugged and tall. The Corps of Discovery traded with Sacagawea's Shoshone and with another Native American nation, the Salish. They got horses to ride through the mountains.

Meriwether Lewis sees the Rocky Mountains.

The trip over the steep mountains was tough. The weather was very cold. It was hard to find food. Many of the men were starving.

The team travels through the mountains.

But the Corps of Discovery kept going. They made it over the mountains. Now they had to cross rivers. They left the horses behind and made canoes. The Corps of Discovery **yearned** to see the Pacific Ocean. In November 1805 the Corps of Discovery finally reached the ocean.

The Corps travels in canoes toward the Pacific.

The **scent** of saltwater filled the air. The men decided to rest. They built Fort Clatsop near the coast in what is now Oregon. They stayed there through the cold, wet winter. Lewis and Clark worked on their maps and scientific records of plants and animals. Then on March 23, 1806, the Corps of Discovery began the trip back home.

The Corps of Discovery sets up camp.

They reached the **docks** of St. Louis on September 23, 1806. It was close to where they had started about $2\frac{1}{2}$ years before. They had traveled nearly eight thousand miles across America! They had mapped rivers and created scientific journals. They had been introduced to many Native American cultures. And they had proved that travel across the continent to the Pacific Ocean was possible.

The journey of the Corps of Discovery comes to an end in St. Louis, Missouri.

The United Sates is a richer nation because of the Louisiana Purchase and men like Meriwether Lewis and William Clark. President Thomas Jefferson also achieved his goal of exploring the American West. These early Americans helped to make the United States of America what it is today.

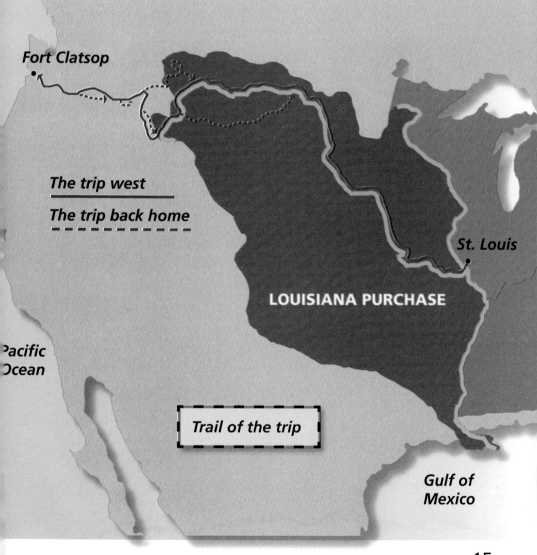

Glossary

docks *n.* platforms built on the shore or out from the shore; wharfs; piers.

migrating *v.* moving from one region to another.

scanned *v.* glanced at; looked over hastily.

scent *n.* a smell.

translated *v.* changed from one language into another.

wharf *n.* a platform built on the shore or out from the shore, beside which ships can load and unload.

yearned *v.* felt a longing or desire; desired earnestly.